Conflicts and
Emotions in Reality

Conflicts and *Emotions* in Reality

War Poetry and *Love Poems*

MILT L. KINS

Printed in the United States of America.

Library of Congress Control Number: 2019904370

ISBN	Paperback	978-1-68536-572-1
	eBook	978-1-68536-573-8

Westwood Books Publishing LLC
Atlanta Financial Center
3343 Peachtree Rd NE Ste 145-725
Atlanta, GA 30326

www.westwoodbookspublishing.com

Contents

Introduction

My name is Sgt. Milton l. king. I was deployed in _Operation Iraqi Freedom_ from March 2003 thru September of 2004. It was hard and troubled times on the deployment. Chaplin Major Kevin Wilkinson told me to write to help deal with everything. I started composing poetry to relax myself. The poetry written in the pages of this book are a combination of combat, spiritual and love poems. It was my way of expressing a newfound talent. This collection of poems will be my first book ever to be published. I actually made it home to my surprise so I'm just finishing what I started. I would like to thank all those people who supported our group during our deployment with support and encouragement. It was that support that kept us going and without I don't think I could have made it.

<u>Sgt. Milton L. King</u>

Dedications

I'd like to dedicate this book of poetry to ***Lenora Riviera (Lily)*** **green angel** and ***Spc. Christopher Taylor***. *Lily* helped to motivate and encourage my spirit while down range in harm's way. I am grateful for every minute of her time. ***Spc. Christopher Taylor*** served and died with our unit there in Iraq. His friendship is greatly missed ever since. His memory will be carried on in our hearts and minds as well as our poems with songs. This book is written in your honor and memory ***"Big T"***

Acknowledgements

I would like to thank all members of **_1165ᵗʰ Military Police Company_** with whom I served in Operation Iraqi Freedom for all their support, encouragement and leadership.

I would like to thank **_Lenora Rivera (Green Angel)_** for all her support, encouragement while deployed to Iraq. Lily you are a great friend and sense of inspiration.

I would like to commend respect to my friend **_Spc.Christopher Taylor_** who did not make it home. His memory and spirit lives on in our hearts and our minds. A poem was written especially for you my friend "**_Big T_**".

I give respect with attention to a major source of inspiration **_Sgt. Jessica A. Sosa_** without whom most of these poems would not have been possible. I thank you for the inspiration and motivation to complete this situation.

I commend and give honor to **_Chaplin Major Kevin Wilkinson_** whose leadership and guidance encouraged me to write and compose while deployed.

I give honor and upmost respect to **_God Almighty_** without whom I wouldn't have had the faith or life to complete this task.

"A Laugh"

A laugh is something that comes from anything.
It could be a ball thrown at a man
That hit so hard he couldn't stand
It comes so easy when things aspire
That with so much action
It makes you prespire.
Things happen and often occur
Let's us know what laughter is for.
Moment happens then we grin somehow
The laughing just never ends.
For a moment we seem to forget
About all the things in our lives we regret.
Laughter is a healthy thing to keep you
pumped on top of your game.
Something silly or called out loud
Everybody hears throughout the
crowd.
That's a laugh it'll keep you going as long as it last's.

A Day As An Mp In The Box

Start the day with juice and a tart
By twelve your praying not to be blown apart
Day's over time to lay down
Then we hear the incoming rounds.
Hagey's chanting some arabic bit.
While we're praying not to be hit.
Info comes of another attack.
Ip's scream for us to strike back. scandal, setup
how can it be.
That's how it is when your an mp

A Sunrise

FOR THE BLESSING OF OUR GREAT GIFTS

A sunrise starts the day it comes up to shine it's
rays. It shines down ever so bright
To make it warm with it's light.
In the cities it comes up
You can see it from just about anywhere
It comes up into the air.
Gases and fuels with drastic fumes
Seem to mess up the view.
Scientists and geologists make
their reports about how we can't stand
In the light no more.
Cancer, blistering from taking to much
Sun in.
All that is something we can prevent.
So something so pretty but yet so mean
That can be reduced with covering.

A Vision Of Love Just Ain'T Enough

A vision of love just ain't enough
With you I'll never give up.
Thought of love as a common thing. a wedding
With a diamond ring. you make a promise on a knee.
I promised to keep her close
We could stay together till we're old
As the days come to pass. the way you
Love will always last.
It might be a call late at night.
Being fussed out to get it right.
It could be a whisper in a phrase.
Just a few words that nobody says.
It could be a reaction or a thought
For something that had been bought.
It's a feeling that we care
For that special someone with whom we share
Our lives, and hearts in so many events
It's been shown and sent. It's made new
It was restored just for you
A song from a man, who's love was gone

All About You

Your eyes such a deep brown takes
A few minutes for me to calm down.
You sit up then you grin
Holding you I don't wanna end
The day start and we part time to go
Do our jobs you never have much
To say as you go on your way.
I catch your attention to say I love
you. That I'm not forgetting.
As you walk away I
Really wish you would stay.
Beauty comes from within to want
You this much it should be a sin
I see you sit ever so quiet
I like to hold you at night.
You'll have a man.
Home with the essential things.
Moments worth cherishing.
All this before you have gone
I'll be here when you come home.

Am I Wrong

Am I wrong for coming home
I've been gone all but eighteen months
I came back to get my life on track
I had constant despair from a life
A wife who really didn't care
She always risked my reputation
And tested my dedication.
It must be something,
She don't wanna see
About the kinda man I try to be
I risked it all while I was gone
Prepared not to make it home.
She never really understood
Things could've been really good.
She gave up and pitched me out.
She drove off without a doubt.
She never really thought alot
How much time I actually got.
I write here to kill my pain
To make my soul free again

An Angel Fell From Heaven

An angel fell from heaven
I caught her in my arms
Right before the ground did any harm
Here I held her, till she came around
As I sat and waited, I didn't make a sound
Her wing were useless. She couldn't even fly
No matter how many times she tried.
I prayed to find a place, she could go
The lord appeared and said
She's here to bring you home
My son that you should know
It might seem crazy at this point
But you'll see as the day goes on
Your life I gave you is so important
Things for you just haven't started
Going in this life things are gonna
Take place .your memory is all that
Will remain you'll find the love
That you seek in your heart
You'll finally have peace that tears you apart

A Story

A story can say so many things.
It starts with a word
Always has an end.
You can make it do so much.
You can make it a person
With alot of luck.
It can tell of fantasies
And so much more.
It can keep you thrilled
Till your eyes get sore.
It can capture your mind
And sense of thought.
It can keep you busy with
Books you bought.
It can be of a love story fair and true.
It can tell how much there you can do.
It all boils down to a simple thought.
That is created and often sought.
A story can create a peace of mind
That is so very hard to find.

A Soldier's Prayer

Oh lord I take my life into your hands
No matter where in this world I stand.
I haven't always done what I should
But by far I did what I could.
I am nothing but a simple man
Who does the best he can.
I stepped into these set of boots knowing what I had to do.
I represent through every attack
With the thought I might not come back.
I can't control where I'm sent.
I don't how long there I will spend.
We have our hard days when it seems like I'm going to get killed.
If not, I return to let my body heal.
Lord today I pray for my soul and the people l affect where I go.
If you can see it in your eyes heaven might be ready when I die.
I'll be coming one way or the other.
The I can join the ranks with my fallen brothers.

A Rose

TO SHOW HOW YOU LOVE IN WORDS
A rose blooms in the spring just in
Time to hear the birds sing.
Petals come out so full of color
The rain falls on it
It couldn't make it any wetter.
Dew gathers up early in the morning
Disappears as the day starts warming.
Prickly thorns on it's stem
You bleed when you touch them.
Something so red in a couple day's is dead.
Coming from someone to show their love.
This gift can't be enough.
They take the flowers ever so polite
The kiss you and hold you tight
One little flower with a prickly stem
It always seems to get to them

As I Lay In This Bed

As I lay in this bed thoughts
Go racing through my head.
Some are loving others are sad
Occurring moments from my past
I try to find some sense of it.
It's hard to keep from throwing a fit.
I see things happening all around me praying not to be let down.
Want to see visions in my life
To keep me doing what's right.
Sadness seems to creep upon me in
The night in my dreams I seem to fight
Can't really make no sense of it
Everything seems to be blank
Have problems sometimes remembering rank.
I feel alone with no place to call my home
Seems like everything I had is gone
Now I feel it's time to roam.
Grab a truck forget my debts
Ride off into the sunset.

Can you believe it

Can you believe it the things we go thru
As we figure out what to do.
We try to change our ways by taking lessons
To become better with a lot less stressing.
Struggles are real as we make decisions
Trying to figure out what we are missing.
The picture we paint from reality this man made hell always
has a story to tell. We learn to deal with what matters
most celebrate our victories with an occasional toast.
Can you believe it seems so tragic
when you truly learn there is no magic?

Ever Had A Dream

Ever had a dream as you sit and think.
In your mind you find images taking shape
About things you desire
At one time or place
You long to have it to hold
It in your grasp
You take it and put up with the crap.
The dream you see seems so vivid
But reality sometimes makes it so rigid.
We take our dreams and try to make them
Come true cause in your life
A dream is all that pulls you through
So once again we lay down our head
As we prepare to go to bed.
Sounds and whispers are all that can be seen
As we sleep and once again start to dream.

Fallen Heroes

TO ALL THOSE LOST IN THE FIGHT

Fallen heroes don't make a sound when their spirit's taken.
They'll no longer be around.
A soldier fights with all his might.
Then his life is lost.
There is no price you can pay to make up the loss.
The friends who had him in their lives now are left alone.
They will be sad now that his spirit gone.
Hearts are often broken when loved ones are lost.
It's the price you pay as the war rages on.
D.O.D. makes a call tells of the mess.
Another soldier has been taken and laid to rest
Gods hands engulf him take him by his side.
His spirit dwells in eternal light.

"Fired"

Fired I think that's
What it's called
Each and every time
I lose my job
Work so hard each day
To keep from being fired
When I get home
My feet are tired
You look to work each day
Put up with all the things they say
Boss comes back to give you a statement
Your no longer needed
No sense in waiting

For You My Love

If the chance for love
Should ever be real then
In time my heart could feel.
For someone for the rest of my life
To come with me and be my wife.
A tear falls from this eye
As I long to be by your side.
In my mind I have these thoughts
Of times we shared and moments caught.
There aint a day that goes by.
I don't want to try to make it last
To make our wrongs be in the past.
I try to make each day of your life
To keep you going so you'll try.
I'll always keep you at your best.
If you love me I can only guess.
Love comes as a surprise caught in your eye's.
I feel the warmth that comes from your heart that let me know
We'll never part

For the love of a woman

For the love of a woman
We give up so much to keep
Them happy when we seem
To act a clutze
For the love of a woman
We seem to give them our heart
Even though they have this way
Of tearing it all apart
For the love of a woman
We find that they make
The meanest spirit's kind
For the love of a woman
Such a docile mind
That we seem to think
They are such a find

For Her

I've never held your hand
Or kissed your face.
Even though we were in the same place.
Beauty so refined and kept within
To want to hold you
Could become a sin.
Never had time to talk
Even see you when you walked
You stop and turn give a smile
To say I didn't see it
I'd be in denial
You have this look
That's just kinda magic
To not be there with you
Could be tragic

For The Love Of A Child

For the love of a child
The things we do
For them as they grew.
That time passes
We view through pane glasses
The pictures of them
In their younger days
How they've changed in so many ways.
For the love of a child
To see them grown
We provide for them a family home

"Grandaddy"

Grandaddy never had a caddie
He really wasn't that smart even though
He gave us everything and his heart
He gave up his schooling and sense to learn
He got a job with wages he could earn
He never said no or turned his family away
He stood strong till his final day
Jaybird was his nickname
It was given to him by his mom
Who watched her baby grow
Into a good man
That he did become
His coat was torn and tattered
It had the occassional old man scent.
The day came god called him home
Up to heaven his spirit went

Gonna Miss this Kiss

Gonna miss this kiss through all I've done
It was your love I thought I had won
When I'm away all you will say
Gonna miss this kiss
In my grasp is where I need you to be
Right here beside of me
As I place my hands on your face
Your there close to be embraced
Gently touch your lips to mine
A feeling so great it can't be defined
Gonna miss this kiss

Gotta Nod For Some Sod

Gotta nod for some sod
Each day as we reach the factor
I climb up into my tractor
Deliveries being made all over town
I'm trying not to act like a clown
Radio plays an ever sweet tune
You'll be getting off soon
Gotta nod for some sod
I drive down the road
Trying to find the proper place
To drop my load.
Transporting grass or some funny kind of weed
Is this what these people really need.
I'm a nodding cause the work be sodding.

He's Some Kinda Heroe

IN MEMORY OF 1165TH MP. CO. O.I.F.

He's some kinda hero world has never known. Trying
to make a right of what is wrong.

I once had a friend never had much to say.
I got the word he'd gone away to some
Foreign country to fight a war.
We all know what he's fighting for.
He was to make amends of a tragic event.
That we could've taken steps to prevent.
I hear off the news soldiers being hit.
Bush had made up a most wanted list.
Saddam had lost his power now is being sought.
It took us a couple months but now he's been caught.

He did his part in this conflict zone.
I heard today he's coming home.

Here Comes Those Mortars Again

Here comes those morters again.
Do you think they'll ever turn them in.
We've been here months never seen it rain.
Survived the heat always did complain.
Every evening about eight o'clock.
Iraqee with a raw deal has to get a shot off
One night got four blasts came close.
They went past bunker drills getting to be
On a regular basis.
Like us bombing up iraqee places.
We often think we have them caught
Try to catch them but they run off.
The first time they did it really wasn't a
Shock.
They wanted revenge for being ticked off
Twenty years of closure kinda makes you
Wanna kill. Somebody frees you wants to make
A deal. our mission changed from precincts
To something else. We hunted I.E.D.'s to
Keep soldier's from getting killed

Here I Arn

Here I am all alone
Since my family has gone.
I feel despair and betrayed
As I sit here counting days.
Rain falls all around.
I can hear each drop as it comes down. The mental anguish from a
Previous love burdens my heart that got shoved.
Here I am talking to myself
About my life that's a living hell.
Personally I'll come around.
I do hope my heart can be found.
Here I am to write it down
To make this heart not drown

Here's A Few Words

Here's a few words that I write
That I hope will excite.
The more words that can be read
Is less words to be said
A few words could change one's fate
He could become someone great
A few words can capture
A moment in time that actually makes sense and rhymes
All it takes is a few words
To make ones day
Then it's done
And you go away
A few words is all it takes
To say your wrong
When you make a mistake
There's a few words

How Special Can It Be

How special can it be
To have someone in your dreams.
To wake in love with someone to hold
For some people
It's a feeling never known.
Somebody by your side
To hold and love till
The day you die.
Always there to remind you of love
To keep you moving through
Life's daily grind.

How To

How to love, how to smile
How to know you've gone the extra mile
How to win, how to sin
How to make your life begin
How to forget, how to regret
How to know it's not your time yet
How to take control
Let it show this one life as it grows.

I Can Mention

I can mention that you have my attention
You caught it the very first day
I know since then I haven't had to much to say
I can mention that every time I hear of you
I can't think only about what I can do
I find myself drawed to your side
My feelings for you I cannot hide
I'm running or feeling, trying to go about my day
I always seem to fumble when you walk my way
I can mention that you took ahold
It seems I've become very bold
I can only mention what you do to me
I long here for your face to see
I can smile ever so faint
When I'm with you there is no complaint
I can mention that you take my breath
A person like you I'll never forget

"It Hurts So"

It hurts so in this life as I go
I really get into it
There is alot of things I don't know
It hurts so to think of my life
With all my failed try's
To be the one to stand strong
To keep spirits high as I go on
It hurts so to think of my wife
What she did to me in this life
It hurts so to forget
The things we did that I regret
It hurts so moving on
When a new life has begun

I won't be there

I won't be there for this occasion
Even though I'm contributing to
The funds you are raising.
I won't be there to hear the songs
Or the poets whose lines run on
I won't be there to share the crowd
To hear the winner's name called aloud
I won't be there physically but the poem
I'm writing will mentally
I won't be there this you can tell
From the title of this poem that I spelled

I'm Moving On

Depression such an anxiety state
Constantly reminded of my mistakes.
Burdens always plague my soul
No matter where I go
In a sense to find myself
Just a little peace of mind.
No more fighting and constant complain
If I stay I'll go insane
Right or wrong doesn't really make it work.
Fussing, being made look like a jerk.
Moving on to put it behind
Drop the hurt from my mind.
Stand up and march again
Time to start back to work will begin
My life will come back into place
Then a smile might appear
Upon this face then it will all be gone I'm moving on

If I Could Love One More Time

I would grab a hold make her mine.
I love her everyday.
Hold her close in a special way.
Cherish every moment that I miss.
Make it up with a kiss.
If and when I had to leave.
The fact I love her she would believe
The phone calls will also start.
Her always being in my heart.
I would love her every moment.
To keep her life going.
As life takes a turn
Things become a mess.
It'll be there to make it the best.
Every time she thinks about me.
It'll be a grin cause she'll always
Know I'm her friend. It seems the
More I write it makes her believe
In herself to achieve.

Im Into You

TO A NEW YORKER IN O.I.F THANKS

I'm into you no matter where you are
or what you do.
I like to hear or be told about things
and places you go.
It can become a strong bond the closer of friends we become.
I like the smile that lingers below your eyes.
Sometimes seems so hard to find.
Stars that reflect in your eyes
once they come out at night.
I'm into you every minute and grateful
for the time you give me.
I long to hear you speak the words of
comfort and wisdom that I need.
I can stand back and watch you sleep
as you take your breathe so deep.
I know you'll be safe from harm
right here in these arms.
The desire to be with you cannot be controlled.
I'll be with you no matter where you go.

In God's Eyes

In god's eye's we are born to lead
Our lives that take shape and form
He watches ever so patiently
In this life that we lead as we earn what we need
Those eyes see all from atop
Each and every time we do wrong
A tear shed's cause of his love
He sits there all the time watching from above
In god's eye's we have a place
That one day
We will rejoice in his grace

Inspired

IF SHE COULD ONLY SEE

Inspired by you
Just by what you do
Everything you represent
Beliefs that get made
Really ain't much more to be said
Inspired to do a little better
As I try to get her.
So much she inspires me to do
If she only knew
Inspired by you something
I can't explain
Seems only by this one woman
Inspired by this spirit I've seen
Who always seems to fill my dreams

Into These Hands

Into these hands you come to me
To tell your hopes and all your dreams.
With an ear I patiently wait
To make sure it's not a mistake.
I see you smile when I come near
I seem to push away all your fears
Though the days we spend apart
I hope someday to win your heart.
Bye and bye as time goes on
I often dream of coming home.
As I fly across the land I see
This world built by man.
It rises high and stretches far
All I see is screeching cars.
Through all the muck and must
You give me hope to not give up
So to you a debt of thanks
For being a friend who understands.

It's A Major

It's a major pain trying not to complain
No matter how depressed I get
It's all the same.
T.V. airs of another slain
To get prisoners freed for political gain
It's a major thing just trying
to live again.
The situation can become major
But still be controlled
As we get in our vehicles
And start to roll.
They're onlooking as he drives away
I'm glad he's gone is what was said
Till we meet again,
Another time, another day
Be safe is all I can say
I'm grateful to get the care
A place to stay while I'm there

"I Did It"

I did it I wrote the whole darn thing
Right here on my computer screen
It started with a few rhyming words
Then I became some kind of nerd
Nouns, verbs and a few adjectives
Throw in some pronouns and it becomes magic
I did it. It made sense about life and all of it's occurring events
To record in time all the things we've done
All the moments and all the fun

"Jesus Said"

Just look to me and believe.
I will make your life be at ease.
If you come to me I will try to teach.
You the words and wisdom to preach.
People will come just to hear the sound
of your voice when you speak.
All the words that will be heard will come directly from me.
Let me come in your heart and walk side by side.
I will hold you up help make you tough.
Be there till you die
People say many things that often make you cry.
It wouldn't be that way if they had me in their life.
My father above has so much love, wisdom he could give
If we announce and bow down in his house
We could live
Now things aren't always gonna be ok
Problems will arise but if you believe
You'll have an eternal life

"Just my love"

Just my love flows from this heart
Even though it's been trampeled
and torn apart
I tried so many different things
To ease the burden and forget
The pain that comes from hurting
Just my love is all I have to offer
to the one I love
Who I always seem to bother
I stand here in suspense
Thinking about myself
Here in the present
Just my love is all I can give to you
Now in this life I live

"Just You"

It's just you every time
I get near you.
I have to take a seat cause
My heart skips a beat.
Rather it be on the tigris
Flying over the seas.
Every time I meet you,
I fall to my knees.
I catch a smile then I kick my heels.
The rest of the day
I'm turning cartwheels.
It's just you who makes me wanna try
The way you make me feel I cannot deny.
Just you make me seem to go beyond
In this life I feel I can do no wrong
Just you thats all it is
One thing I wanna kiss

Just A Little

TO A FRIEND WHO UNDERSTANDS

Just a little love will get me through each day as I think of you.
Just a little farther on my way
I think in my heart you can always stay
Just a little closer we have become
Being together has been so much fun.
Just a little more space to bring it in
Here this relationship will never end
Just a little smarter than before
As I keep coming back for more
Just a little thing that I do
Because I'm in love with you

Just So Much

LO-VE FOR SOMEONE SPECIAL

Just so much a man can do
when he falls in love with you.
He hurts when your not there
to show him that you really care.
Just so much a man can give
to his wife as they live.
He comforts her when sad sits with her
through times that are bad.

Just so much strength a man
can show to let his love know.
He puts out a constant strain and
takes to himself the load of pain.

Just so much wisdom a man can posess
to help him pass life's test.
He trys to guide ever so right
and keep her safe every night.

Kaitlin

TO MY BABY SIX YEARS OLD AND GROWING

A little girl was given life. Born into the light
I saw her smile. the very first day
I knew, I'd never let her get away
As the days of her life took toll
That little girl started to grow
First came hair, a couple teeth
She was crawling around on all four feet
Started walking then said her first words.
The prettiest sound I ever heard.
Every time I see her smile
I remember back about this child.
How gods blessed and brought her here.
I was chosen to be there.
Every time she's threatened in her life.
I can feel the fear in her eyes.
Let her grow aint no place she can't go
Years just fade away, she no longer stays
Finds love then we part
She will always be in my heart

Life And Love As We Live It

There once was a girl who had grace and
beauty. She came from nowhere just to see
Me. I saw her walk up to say hello minutes
Before I had to go. As I left and we
Departed I saw the look of disappointment as
we parted.
She slowly hung her head and sighed all at once she started to cry.
At this moment in this very place I could
See the love on her face.
The look she gave me with a constant stare
I knew I couldn't go anywhere.
A women with such beauty stands right here
before me.
I reach down to give her a kiss.
A moment I don't wanna miss.
As we touch and the feelings begin
I don't want this moment to ever end.

Love With Distance And Emotions

For a love from afar who I don't really know where you are

I'd like you to come with me.
We can travel far across the seas.
I promise to make it a timely event.
It'll be worth every cent.
See the world at a steady pace.
Cherish each moment as it takes place.
Songs and jokes will be told.
Day's will pass while time goes.
It's hard to say how it will go.
Each day feels great.
You there in my embrace.
No need to say a thing.
Your heart desires a ring.
You don't want just another fling.
Tell a story with a grand ending.
A lot of love with no pretending.
He'll take a knee
Make the commitment to marry thee.
It's done the moment is caught.
Your love is all to be sought

My Baby

Such a beautiful face that I see
As my baby stands here in front of me.
I've never known a love for someone
Could have grown so much but
Yet be so little
A love one has can be quite brittle.
My baby I have seen so many times
As she comes in each night.
My baby always working hard being sure
Not to get fired. She works herself practically to death
Getting things done with every breath
My baby gives all then she's tired
Here I wait so she can be desired
I know it's all worthwhile
When I see her smile

My Dear

She sits and waits hopefully that one day
That they will meet.
She talks of herself job, kids
How she feels. She says no one has ever
Loved her that would last.
They leave her world begins to crash.
If it couldn't be true.
Someone is in love with you.
He brings something into her life that
Makes her laugh, forget how to cry.
Her dreams and heart all start soaring.
Her life doesn't seem so boring.
This puts a twinkle in her eye.
Since this friend came into her life

My Friend T

IN MEMORY OF CHRIS TAYLOR
HIS NAME WAS TAYLOR WAS BIG AND WIDE.
HE KICKED LIKE A HORSE AND LOVED TO FIGHT.
SOME PEOPLE TRY TO BE HEROS THAT I'VE SEEN.
NO ONE COMPARES TO MY FRIEND "T".
KEVLAR WORN UPON HIS HEAD HAD
DILLIGAF WRITTEN ON IT'S BAND.
INITALED WORDS ONLY HE COULD UNDERSTAND.
HE WAS SERIOUS MADE NO JIVE ALWAYS
THERE TO SAVE A LIFE. HE COULD SIGHT
A TARGET FROM A THOUSAND YARDS.
HE COULD RUN ALL DAY NEVER TIRE.
ONE NIGHT ENEMY CAME IN SIGHT
AND "T" GOT INTO THE FIGHT. HE
CAME AROUND GOT SHOT DOWN.
WE FELT SAD FOR OUR FRIEND
THOUGHT HE HAD MET HIS END.
HE SAT UP AND SPOKE "MAN THEM
HAGEYS GOTTA GO".
THE DAY CAME WE HEARD A BLAST
DIDNT KNOW IT WOULD BE
"Ts" last.
A GREAT MAN WITH A HEART SO SWEET
ALWAYS GIVE WHEN IN NEED.

My Grandmother

My grandmother was dearest to me
She was there to comfort me.
She would keep me in her sights
She'd scold me if I didn't do right.
Time put wrinkles on her head
Her hair slowly turned gray
Through her patients and tears
She never turned us away
Things take from us
The things we love the most.
Our hearts will be with her
Now that she goes.
She will dwell in peace now
that her life has come to cease
We will cherish every moment in our hearts
The day has come for us to part
The memories left in our hearts
They'll be there to keep us moving on
Let us know to whom we belong.

Oh Lord Im Waiting

TO LIFT THE SPIRITS OF GRACE CHAPEL

Oh lord I'm waiting I'm here for the taking.
How I long to stand before you.
Oh how I adore you.
A prayer that I make my spirit you'll take.
Into your hands my soul I give.
In your house forever I'll live.
I sing praise to you almighty.
I pray you don't deny me.
I will tell of your stories to people before me.
My heart has seen grief that has made disbelief.
I prayed upon my knees and there you saved me.

Oh Sweet Thing

Oh sweet thing would you like a ring
It can only be a promise from me
To care here for eternity
It will call for a few long hours
As we try to share the power
Oh sweet thing I'd think you would care
With me being over here
Oh sweet thing I long
To look upon your face
As I sit here in this place
Oh sweet thing how can it be
To want you here beside of me

On The Wing Of An Angel

A promise was made
I'll always remember the words
That she said.
She came with her wings to take me away
To a better place.
She came in glory
She descended down before me
She came without word
Give love and affection.
Here we made a connection.
She promised me love
Life free of worry, and sighs
This angel had a smile on her face.
I tried my best to stand in place.
She walked up eyes were a glow
Her great beauty was all she showed
She spoke words softly into my ear
I burst into tears.
She gave me courage to be a man
My inspiration to be the best I can

Once I Walk And I Talk

Dawn comes and we stand here looking upon our lives.
How we always seem to fuss and fight.
The battle rages on.
I know our love is gone.
The feeling will never be back in this home.
I can see the pain and oppression
That looms on your face.
Things I have done that nothing can replace
A spirit of love once dwindled
The flame has now kindled.
What am I still here for
If you don't love me anymore
Tomorrow a brand new day
The sun will come up.
I think of the good times
When we were still in love.
You might not want to have me
Hold me by your side.
You can push me away out of your sight. Once I walk and I talk
You gonna cry like never before

"Our World"

Our world in which we live
Changes and seldom gives
Our world has grown so big that we can't
Really hold it all in
It stretches as far as the eye can see
So many miles from sea to sea
You can travel and see it all
From a plane it seems quite small
Our world is always growing
Becoming faster and always knowing

One Light In The Night

One light in the night
Is all I can see
Blurred vision can be slightly hard
Trying to make your way
You become quite tired
See the light as it shines ahead
Let's you know your not yet dead
One light in the night
Shines so bright
To bring you back
Let you know where your at

Our President

TO THE ONE WHO LEADS US

A man who leads a nation
Always involved with litigations.
Media always giving him hell
Every word he says, they try to spell.
He can't have a moment in his life
That isn't seen or viewed by someones sight.
Reports and decisions have to be made
About someone who had something to say.
War comes and goes.
Casualty rate is all that shows. Fighting to bring about a change
We try to keep things from being the same.
Stress from upcoming events wondering
If his term in office will end.
He tours the country from state to state
He fights opponents in a heated debate
Election draws near inside there is some fear.
Every word he makes to be said
If it ain't right soldiers wind up dead.

"Politics"

TO THOSE WHO LIVE TO RUN

Bush toured the country
Decided to take a break.
Kerry makes the statement iraq
Was a mistake.
Polls come back to tell a different note.
Each candidate strives hard
To earn more votes.
We sit back and take it all in
As the day for election settles in.
Bush lets us know troops in a few years will gradually come back.
Kerry sits and talks of the past.
Move on, move up with politics
It's never enough

She's On Her Way

She's on her way when I called had alot
Of nice things to say
From the call got a statement seems my angel
Has found herself an engagement
Looks love has found it's way back into her
Life and somebody desires her for a wife
Well I guess when you are alone
Somebody has to keep you strong
So I guess this means this case is closed
Because this angel has found itself
A new home

She's Some Kind of Hero

For SGT. Jessica Sosa O.I.F. 1 2004

She's some kind of hero
For the world to see
This is what she'll always be
Carry a gun or leading a team
Never having a doubt it seems.
Taken oh so far away to a land to stay.
Fear with depression after time
Starts to appear
In her heart her loved ones are near.
Hard to smile under such stress
Pushing hard never getting much rest
Always trying to be ready for a fight
As she works each day and night.
Family seems to cheer her up
As they send her needed stuff.
She knows her baby just a phone call away
Even though
He really ain't got many words
He can say

Simply

Simply we try to go do as much
That we can in this life
We run life's ever so heavy gauntlet
Living in it the memories taunt me
Simply we make all our daily needs
People still have obssesive greed
Moments happen to bring back things from our past
Recent events that never really last
Simply we wait and plan upcoming events
We make it special with invitations sent
Simply we clear our thoughts
We review those moments caught Simply
We take on a whole new plan
Live this life the best we can
Simply we learn to love
Have a little faith in the man above
Simply all you can do is try to live
Enjoy each day of your life
That was a gift

So Much I Dread

So much I dread on this road
That lies ahead
It holds so much inside
That each moment comes as a surprise
Emotions seem to find a way to drive
Themselves right back into your life
So much I dread it seems in my heart
Including my dreams
This road on which my life seems to ride
My heart and soul seem to have died
So much I dread inside my head
I pray not to wind up dead

Some Heores Are Born
Others Are Trained The
Memory Left Will Remain

All over the country from guam to vietnam
Soldiers are fighting for their uncle sam.
They felt heat and dust
From the middle east.
They survived attacks from I.E.D.'s. several had gotten injured
Some had been killed
We keep on coming of our own free will.
Nearly two hundred years,
We've been fighting for some cause.
We had some serve others we had lost.
We completed the mission
No matter what the cost.
People look to us for inspiration
They gather from us hope and admiration.
Soldiers have fought and died
There families mourn and cry.
We complete our mission with little or no need.
Sometimes we become prisoners
Who will never be freed
We stand together, we have strength
there ain't nothing we can't defend.

Something Great

Something great is all we want to take.
It comes slowly gets to be fast
Here it takes off
How long will it last
Something great is how you feel
Every time you make a good deal.
It is so many things unexplained.
It's just how well you are trained. Written, sung or screamed
Out to let people know what your about
Something great is what you have earned
As your life makes certain turns.
Only one life has been given
Here you learn to start living. Enjoying each day
Having something nice to say
What we learn is to have fate cause
Things come easy when your something great

Take Me Back Where I Belong

I'm just a man with two hands
Standing with an arabic friend.
We're trying to understand
Why we were brought to this foreign land
I've been in this country to long
Take me back where I belong.
A many days spent sweating away
Thinking about our lives in another place.
Our hearts melt in place
We see the pain and suffering on the children's face.
We bring peace to a country
That has never seen nothing but war.
They never seem to learn
What we came here for.
We try to bring aid and carry out
What the general has said.
Siver bird come down from above
Take us home to the family we love

The Bartender

TO THE ONE WHO MIXES MY DRINK

They mix the drinks that we buy
Always smile and say hi.
They bring to mind a sense of peace
To give your mind a way to release
All the things and stress in our lives
We seem to get alcohol in a bottle or
A cup, to much will mess you up.
They deal with each spirit
Giving them what they want.
To many drinks then help them home.
Eight to ten hours on their feet
After working all night they are beat.
We tend to forget exactly what they do
When they stand right there in front of you
I guess you can say they give you peace
In a bottle for which you pay.
All that from a little bar, you can drive to with your car.
The bartender can give so many things.
If you wait you can even sing. The job isn't for everyone
Somebody has to get it done.

"The Debate"

The debate went down
two candidates face off.
To prove to the world
Who is best for the job.
Each conjures up a different story
To ditch the other one
As they stand there before you.
Standing there trying to make sense
As they talk about all
Of our political events.
One has already been running controlling our fate
While the other keeps saying Iraq was a mistake.
Each person has a plan
To make the world safe again.
Proof to be the best man
Who is gonna do for us
All that he can

"The Dwindling Spirit"

The dwindling spirit looms in the room
It seems possessed with so much gloom
It holds so much hatred within
It scorns people whose lives it's in
The spirit watches with a scornful heart
It does it's best to tear apart
It strikes fear in the soul of every man
They run and hide the best they can
The spirit makes a rattling sound
It even sometimes shakes the earthly ground
Man envelopes each moment
with so much fright
He can't never sleep at night
The dwindling spirit will always be around
He is here
You can find him in every town

"The Eye Doctor"

You can only see through these eyes
The vision we see can't be denied
The eye doctor takes a course to learn
Credit hours are the things he's earned
Degrees hang all over the walls
To do his job patients sometimes stall
Faith and training is all he's got
To get the job done right
Rather it be civilian or military personell
He has proven to be the best in his field
As he sits back and watches
His patients heal

"The Lawyer"

The lawyer who works a case
Who finds means to convict
When there is no trace
Find the truth enforce what's right
As he prepares to make a fight
Defend or become a plaintiff
Just making sure the facts and truth
Are spilled
Make the court believe in the facts
To rule in truth as they
Sit there in the booth

"The Teacher"

The teach us all they know
To develop our minds as we grow
Always smile as we come to class
Even though we do seldom sass
They teach such great things we need
How to be right and do good deeds
It can be english with nouns and verbs
It could be math with no words
Language arts or even health
Things you write about feelings felt
The teacher has so much for you to learn
In this life the things you earn
In teaching we become one of the best
In the end god will take care of the rest

The Librarian

TO SAYERS "HUWEE FOR DEWEY"

Dewey with decimals for books on shelves
To help keep them organized
So they can sale.
They mark and tape on each end
All that has to happen before
Shelving can begin.
The librarian puts them in their place. Some by numbers
To keep plenty of space.
Authors by name
Who had quite some fame.
Fiction or non-fiction is it real
Just here to read, that's the deal
Checked out books, ain't in
All that is the job of the librarian. Everything put in a spot
Either has a number or they forgot.
Taped, marked and completely in line all
That takes up their time.
Books needing to be put In a assigned spot to keep
The librarian a job.

The Life That Was Given

The life that was given for us to fullfill
We live it each day with the upmost thrill
We take in the moments with stride
As we go on through the days of our lives
Sometimes we take this for granted
As things happen that makes sudden changes
We're born with nothing at all when
In this world we are actually quite small.
Of all the places and events through this
Life we are sent we learn to love and appreciate more the things
We often achnored.
So in close to make the statement true
To record the things that you do
This life is a one time shot to show
The world exactly what you got.
So make the best of what you are and
With this life you may go very far.

The Lilly Beside The Tree

FOR A GREEN ANGEL WITH LUCK

There once was a lilly beside a tree
I dug it up and took it with me
I brought it home to a real nice place.
I kept it close in my embrace.
I gave it love, made it grow.
The lilly sprouted like never before
Her petals grew long, color so radiant
She leaned toward the sun for bathing
I bought her a light
To shine upon her place.
To keep her strength and beauty from fading
I kept that lilly close to me
I kept all her seeds.
I planted many more, watched them grow
None of these flowers will ever be
Sweet as that first lilly by the tree.
Time makes thing's slowly aging
Our minds and bodies go through stages
Like the lilly beside the tree
I hope one day someone will care for me.

The Poet

Written words that form a sentence
That come together
To hold a meaning.
Phrases or paragraphs
wrote in so many ways
That come together as an essay.
He uses words to make a point
About certain people
He has known.
So many things with words
That he can do
That bids his time
In this life
He goes through

The Policemen

TO MY FRIENDS ON THE FORCE

At the precinct is where he resides
he comes to work each night.
A pistol with a badge comes with vest
If you work hard to pass all their tests.
You are given a partner and car
Hoping that you go very far.
Days go by there you work
You try your best not to get hurt.
Each day seems to be challenging
While your out traveling
You police the streets to make things right
Each day before you go home at night.
Tickets are often wrote
To people who the law they broke. Sometimes it's easy
sometimes it's h***
We have had some killed.
Twenty for a pension and a check
Then relax and try to forget.
All that to be a policemen in the fight
Who every day risks his life.

The Preacher

The preacher comes into the church
To get his sermon ready to be heard
Faith and goodness fills his sight
As he prepares for his night
He reads a few verses as time passes
While he's rehearsing
He prays to god to give him faith
Let's him know he's thankful for being saved
He gets loud to the crowd beliefs are known
It seems for a moment the evil is gone
Sermon is over message is done now it's time for us to go
home

The Vet

The vet is someone who serves.
He learns to have guts
with alot of nerve.
He trains to be at his best
Just like all the rest.
Conflict, explosions
In a combat zone
Learn to make his beliefs known.
Always prepared ready to fight
ain't afraid to give his life.
Through the wars rank has grown
never knowing if he'd make it home.
Twenty years and a letter
hoping and praying
The job get's better.
Let the family know
That the support of him
In his mind he can live.

This Gun Of Vengeance I Show

People come in front of my sights
While I'm riding low.
I always strike fear into their souls
With this gun of vengeance I show.
I see them riding in cars
They're on street corners and inside bars
They look with hatred and regret.
They attack every chance they get.
They see me as I come by.
They don't wanna try but if so
I will take their souls
With this gun of vengeance that I show.
The people attack us every night.
We get up prepare to fight.
They bring us violence and grief
More days added with no sign of relief
I set up position. I sight them in
I wait for the action to begin.
They set up their tubes prepared to fight
One by one I take their life

"To Much Of A Hunk
To Be A Drunk"

I'm to much of a hunk to be a drunk
No matter how long I've been gone
I try not to drink cause in my mind
I can't really think.
The hangovers tend to last for sometime.
The night before the women were fine.
I stand in front of the mirror
It seems like the view could be clearer.
People look upon me as a crazy vet
Who ain't quite caught up with reality yet.
Reality sets in I wake up
Boy don't this really suck.
I hear some people playing out loud
It's really disturbing
It makes me wanna shout

To Be An American

To be an american
Who does what's right
Who protects his country in every fight
He always stands strong and proud
He looks that way in front of a crowd.
He keeps his beliefs strong day and night
He defends his country with all his might
He never backs down or runs away
He never has to many words to say
To be an american
In this place we live
Our military preserves the freedom
They give.
To be an american
In the land of the brave
A flag of red, white, and blue
That will always wave.

Top

Take a man who always trys to be a friend
Who deals with lives.
No matter what the situation
Always gives full dedication
Each problem that comes about
Always around to take it out.
Helps soldiers who are in need
To be the one who does the good deed
Injured, shot or torn apart
He seems to show a heart.
A soldier to a point who don't care.
It's good to know, someone is there.
Be a friend treat them to a game
Pay their way and don't complain
Drink a few and shout out loud
As we sit inside the crowd.
Catch a ball sign your name
As we start to leave the game
It's an honor to have met this friend
As my civilian life begins

Trying To Forget

Misery and sadness fills the halls
Dark scary shadows
Loom on the walls
Long wailing sounds can be heard
Through the night
As things get stirred
Nightmares of scary events
That life has seemed to present
Depression leads to anger
That turns to fear
Every time the moments get near.
Things happen that take us back
To tragic times in our past
Positive thoughts try to take hold
All the bad memories we let go.

Under Fire

Under fire we came in
Moments after an attack begin
Direct hits taken on each side
In our hearts we desperately cried
Under fire we fought back
To kill the one's who attacked
Under fire we made a pack
That each of us would come back.
Strapped with lead there in the fight
We fought the enemy till they died
Under fire people change their fate
With a prayer they find a mate
Under fire with incoming lead
So many spirits wind up dead

Used To

Used to laugh, used to smile,
Used to think about you for awhile.
Used to love you so much
Before things happened and I gave up
Used to to dream of our lives we shared
Back when you really cared.
Used to really care about you where you were at
If you were ever coming back.
Used to worry about your life
back when you were my wife
Used to really feel
But times has passed
My wounds have healed

"When I Look At You"

To hear your voice, such a beautiful noise
I know you are the right choice
Just a look is all it took
I can't stop thinking of you
I see so much love, I just wish
I could be there to see you wake up,
Watch you sleep, be there when you eat
It's a love that could become
Together it might be some fun
When I look at you, I see your eyes
That possess so much mystery inside
So much beauty kept within
A prayer answered for any man
I'd hold you by my side have you there
With me every night. when I look
At you I see us kiss
A moment that I cannot resist.
I put my hand around your waist,
Pull you close into my embrace,
All that love a lady can possess.
I know now she not like the rest

We Won'T Stop

The convoy started rolling about six A.M.
We got rolling good then the attack begin
Bullets flying all around.
Sargent yelling to get down.
We got the enemy in our sights.
We won't stop till there no one
left to fight.
We flanked their position trying to make them dead.
Rounds were being fired at our heads.
Backup arrived just in the nick of time.
We had four tanks and a helicopter in the sky.
Theirs eye's got big as drums.
One by one they started to run.
After the attack we had an after action review.
Lt. got mad really came unglued.
We didn't lose any time
Get those who committed the crime.
You do wrong we'll put you where ya belong.
After an attack like this you really get upset but a day like this
You won't forget.

Whispers From An Angel

I often have problems before I go to sleep
It's there I start to dream.
She lays down beside me I pull her near.
She keeps me happy and full of cheer.
Whispers from an angel takes me by the heart.
The dreams she creates
Tears me all apart.
She comes to sit beside me
In my favorite place.
There my heart she takes. The feeling she creates
Fills me with desire like
Water falling upon a flower.
Into our bed we go there she tells
Me what I need to know.
She talks of undying love. A promise to be made
One day we both will wed.
She speaks of comfort
Time spent apart
She let's me know I'm in her heart

You Are My Love Of Whom
I Can'T Get Enough

The first night we met.
I'll never forget
I ran into you so upset.
You didn't smile or even try to grin
That is where our love began
The first date didn't go great
Car wouldn't start and ended up an hour late
Patiently you waited there for me
How was I to know with you I'd always be
Days turned into months and suddenly
They were years
Seemed like the greatest times
Cause you were here.
Moments we had together are very fond
But our love just keeps going on

You Are The One

You are the one who I count on
You give me strength
to rise like the sun.
If I'm down and your around
You are certain to act a clown
Make the frown just disappear.
To hide and run from the fears
You are the one there near
Who shows belief in me with faith.
It keeps me going really makes my day.
You are the one who believes in me
To be the best man I can be

Adjust Fire

Deep in depression I know I've been stressing
the world has gone to shit.
Sitting around and feeling down life's puzzle don't fit.
Situations are untold.
Moments we embrace and hold.
Ordered to the border, in demand coming to our land.
They on a mission know they been wishing.
Life's just outta of hand.
Adjust fire recalibrate saving lives before it's too late.
Migrant groups on the march to make the
border where they can cross.
We understand freedom to gather a lot but
not access to the country we got.
Group grows in size as it makes its way.
We gather by brigade pulling security to block their way.
Access to the border won't be gained by any that makes a stand.
Trump makes it known we will defend
our borders with force shown.
Groups can turn or be retreated no harm done or anyone defeated.

Gotta jump for trump

Obama gave us $599 on a 1099.
Bush gave us a push.
Trump stood to lead and the news begins to read.
Gotta jump for Trump some say Trump has become a disorder
because of his policies and views with with our borders.
Illegals being deported just after we no longer support it. Gotta
jump for Trump he made a decision to inflict a travel ban of
Muslims who come into our land.
Worked with Korea to end the war bring peace unlike before.
Minutes passed moments changed the world
became safer under this man.
Gotta jump for Trump foreign policy got resolved
programs made problems solved.
Serve his country under oath to defend couldn't be a better man.
Gotta jump for Trump paper reads stormy weather for
Trump administration all to question his reputation.
That really upset my president but it isn't
quite thru still got a job to do.
Gotta jump for Trump

Made in the USA
Columbia, SC
13 August 2022